A DRAGON IN THE SANDPIT

Level 1H

Written by Louise Goodman
Illustrated by Inna Chernyak

What is synthetic phonics?

Synthetic phonics teaches children to recognise the sounds of letters and to blend (synthesise) them together to make whole words.

Understanding sound/letter relationships gives children the confidence and ability to read unfamiliar words, without having to rely on memory or guesswork; this helps them progress towards independent reading.

Did you know? Spoken English uses more than 40 speech sounds. Each sound is called a *phoneme*. Some phonemes relate to a single letter (d-o-g) and others to combinations of letters (sh-ar-p). When a phoneme is written down it is called a *grapheme*. Teaching these sounds, matching them to their written form and sounding out words for reading is the basis of synthetic phonics.

Consultant

I love reading phonics has been created in consultation with language expert Abigail Steel. She has a background in teaching and teacher training and is a respected expert in the field of Synthetic Phonics. Abigail Steel is a regular contributor to educational publications. Her international education consultancy supports parents and teachers in the promotion of literacy skills.

Reading tips

This book focuses on:
cvc, cvcc, ccvc compounds
(c=consonant, v=vowel) such as 'sandpit'

Tricky words in this book

Any words in bold may have unusual spellings or are new and have not yet been introduced.

Tricky words in this book:

the he lady what this they wants to king I'll says her wave smiled boatman

---

Extra ways to have fun with this book

• After the reader has read the story, ask them questions about what they have just read:

Who was the person in the sandpit?
What did the lady hit the dragon with?

• Make flashcards of the focus graphemes. Ask the reader to say the sounds. This will help reinforce letter/ sound matches.

Let me tell you, getting sand inside this armour makes it very itchy!

A pronunciation guide

This grid contains the sounds used in the story and a guide on how to say them.

s as in sat	a as in ant	t as in tin	p as in pig
i as in ink	n as in net	c as in cat	e as in egg
h as hen	r as in rat	m as in mug	d as in dog
g as in get	o as in ox	u as in up	l as in log
f as in fan	b as in bag	j as in jug	v as in van
w as in wet	z as in zip	y as in yet	k as in kit
qu as in quick	x as in box	ff as in off	ll as in ball
ss as in kiss	zz as in buzz	ck as in duck	

Be careful not to add an 'uh' sound to 's', 't', 'p', 'c', 'h', 'r', 'm', 'd', 'g', 'l', 'f' and 'b'. For example, say 'fff' not 'fuh' and 'sss' not 'suh'.

Nick is in **the** sandpit.

He is by himself.

A **lady** is in the sandpit!

But **what** is **this**?

A dragon is in the sandpit.

"Huff-puff!"

The dragon **wants to** get the lady!
"Buzz off!" says the lady.

A **king** is in the sandpit!

"**I'll** help!" **says** the king.

"Not yet!" says the lady.

She hits the dragon with
her handbag.

Then a **wave** hits the sandpit!

The dragon, the lady and the
king are swept off!
"Help! Quick!"

A **boatman** is in the sandpit.

They all go back to land.

But what is this?

Dad is in the sandpit!

"Was it fun?" says Dad.

"Yes!" said Nick, and **smiled**
to himself.

OVER 48 TITLES IN SIX LEVELS
Abigail Steel recommends...

Other titles to enjoy from Level 1

Bad Rat

978-1-84898-277-2

The Best Gift

978-1-84898-396-0

Gran and Bret's Trip

978-1-84898-547-6

Some titles from Level 2

Wish Fish

978-1-84898-386-1

Chuck and Duck

978-1-84898-387-8

Pink Bunny

978-1-84898-550-6

Let's go to the Swings

978-1-84898-549-0

Some titles from Level 3

Bart's Go-Cart

978-1-84898-552-0

Queen Ella's Feet

978-1-84898-398-4

Puff Flies

978-1-84898-399-1

The Pop Duet

978-1-84898-551-3

An Hachette UK Company
www.hachette.co.uk

Copyright © Octopus Publishing Group Ltd 2012
First published in Great Britain in 2012 by TickTock, a division of Octopus Publishing Group Ltd,
Endeavour House, 189 Shaftesbury Avenue, London WC2H 8JY.
www.octopusbooks.co.uk

ISBN 978 1 84898 554 4

Printed and bound in China
10 9 8 7 6 5 4 3 2 1